Gifts Bestowed

poetry by

Norma
Beversdorf-Rezits

Anne Beversdorf,
Editor

Gifts Bestowed

Poetry by

Norma Beversdorf-Rezits

Anne Beversdorf,
Editor

Stariel Press

Stariel Press
Austin, Texas
www.stariel.com
StarielPress@stariel.com

Honoring Mom, her secret poetry, and her gift of allowing us to find these gems after her passing.

Contents

Preface

This is the second of what may be a four-volume posthumous series of unrevealed poetry by my mother, Norma Beversdorf-Rezits.

The first poem in this book has special resonance for her family and loved ones. She appears to have recognized the power of her poetry to relieve the pain of her passing and to give us new ways of understanding this world and the next.

Coincidentally, this second book is being published within weeks of the performance of a group of songs for tenor, commissioned by Vicki King for her husband, tenor Thomas King, and based on Norma's poetry. The songs were composed by Lauren Bernofsky, and the song series is titled ***The Secret Philosopher.*** You can hear them on YouTube and find them by searching Secret Philosopher. The printed music can be obtained by contacting
Lauren Bernofsky at
lbernofsky@LaurenBernofsky.com.

Anne Beversdorf

Norma Beversdorf-Rezits:
An Introduction

by
Anne Beversdorf

NBR's Poetic Work

This book of poetry has an unusual provenance. Because I was the only person who knew that Norma Beversdorf-Rezits had been a serious poet her entire life, everyone else was surprised by the winter coat box full of poems discovered under her bed after her death.

The poetry in this collection was taken from several sources of Norma's carefully preserved works. These include

1. Her own curated diary compilation of several hundred poems gathered in 2004.
2. Three chapbooks of poetry given to her parents as holiday gifts
3. SEVEN folders of poems she gathered in groups in the winter coat box under her bed.

(I didn't dare explore the dozen-plus handwritten notebooks, mainly be-cause her handwriting was known for illegibility!)

After receiving two beautiful poems from Mom over a decade ago, I asked her if she had kept the poetry she'd been writing all her life. She answered "Oh, yes!" When asked where, she answered "In a box under my bed." Asked if I could see them. she said "After I'm dead!" Which is what happened.

The poems in this volume represent a small fraction of the approximately 700 poems Norma saved over her lifetime. If you knew her, you will think back to those occasions when she broke out of her good-humored, chatty manner and offered you a little glimpse of the soul who could write with such art and depth.

Biography

Norma Beversdorf-Rezits' life was both ordinary and unusual. Norma Beeson was born September 9, 1924, in San Antonio, Texas, an only child to loving parents. She received her BA in Music with a piano specialty from the University of Texas in Austin and married Thomas Beversdorf in 1945. Norma lived a conventional mid-century life as the wife of a classical music composer and professor, and as mother of their children.

Before maternity she taught music in the public school system in Texas. Later, she taught preschoolers and gave piano lessons to adults in Bloomington, Indiana, where Thomas Beversdorf was on the faculty at the Indiana University School of Music (now the Jacob School of Music). He became chair of both the Composition Department and the Brass Instruments Department.

Norma was known for her gracious charm and the numerous parties she gave celebrating her husband's music performances and honors. More privately, she had a sharp and often dry sense of humor that is sometimes evident in her poetry.

Norma's life and poetry were affected by more than just the events that most wives and mothers encountered in the mid-20th century. She had three daughters, the third of whom died at age two in an accidental drowning at home. She immediately had two more children, sons, the oldest of whom is profoundly autistic. He was born when few MDs in the world even knew what that was.

Norma rejected advice that he be placed in an institution, convinced she could "reach" him. Despite her son being non-verbal until age seven, she spent ten hours each day "training" him (literally saying "I didn't teach him. I trained him"). She made up her own methods, both supporting and making use of his strengths rather than trying to make his weaknesses reach traditional educational standards.

When her second son was born, Norma's husband invited both of her parents to move from Texas to Indiana on a piece of land he deeded to them. There they could live across the street from their daughter's family and their grandchildren.

Norma was an early practitioner of yoga, again privately, at home, and had three of her children by natural childbirth in the early 1960's. She was an avid reader of Paul Valery, Paul Tillich, Erich Fromm, Martin Buber, Soren Kierkegaard, Eric Hoffer, and Thomas Merton. I was aware of her reading the poetry of T.S. Eliot, and e.e. cummings. I'm sure there were others.

Thomas Beversdorf died of asthma in 1981 when their sons were still in high school. Tom and Norma were both in their fifties at the time. Within a few years both of her parents also passed. When Tom died, Norma was working on her Master's Degree in Special Education. After his death and on the completion of her Master's degree she started teaching in a small town near Bloomington. When it became clear that the district neither cared about nor supported special education at a minimal legal level, Norma left that position.

Because of Norma's unprecedented efforts, her autistic son continued to defy expectations and earned a B.S. in computer science. Ultimately he would find a stable job as a government computer programmer and programming manager. Her second daughter is a retired Fine Arts Librarian from Avery Library, Columbia University. Her youngest son is an MD specializing in neurology. I am the oldest child, and I am a professional western and Vedic astrologer.

Norma Beversdorf-Rezits

After her sons finished college Norma travelled all over the world and enjoyed gathering with friends at card games, dinners, concerts and plays. When she was in her early eighties she moved to Meadowood, a vital, university-related senior living center. There she met and fell in love with Joseph Rezits, who had been a colleague of her late husband, and whose deceased wife had given cello lessons to Norma's autistic son decades earlier. Joseph Rezits had been chairman of the Piano Department at the IU Music School and still performed regularly.

Norma and Joseph thrilled family and friends with their joyful marriage at 88 years of age. They both declared that this was "the love of my life." After seven years of love and mutual support, Joseph died in November of 2019 and Norma followed him in May of 2020.

The Poetry of Life

In Norma's poetry, complex ideas are expressed in minimal words. Almost none of her poems are over one page in length. Many are less than twenty words. We see here a deeply spiritual and independent woman, outwardly living a life that conformed to the norms and expectations of the mid-20th century world but defining her own awareness and individuality in her private world of poetry. Her love of ambiguity, her unwillingness to label things Good or Bad, her ability to see universality in seemingly disparate views are all evident in her work.

It becomes obvious, in retrospect, that this work was a necessity for her strongly independent identity, and that her poetry is the work of her soul, writ small but powerfully, serving the needs of her deepest self.

This book of poetry offers a glimpse into Norma Beversdorf-Rezits' extraordinary hidden life. We celebrate her unexpected gift to her family, friends, and to the world.

August 2020

Poetry

I bequeathed
Quantities
Never
Released
in turn
an empty hull
has carved an ache
which quickens still
as parts of you
Return again.

Norma Beversdorf-Rezits

the only gift
is that bestowed
all others crumble
when exposed

Norma Beversdorf-Rezits

Norma Beversdorf-Rezits

Understanding,
So great
Yet
Crippling
Sometimes –
Please let
Sweet creatures
Fly free.

Norma Beversdorf-Rezits

Sometimes
you quietly fall
upon my face –
as from the sun
so lightly placed.
I cannot feel
your weight,
yet from
eternity
you come.

Norma Beversdorf-Rezits

Do you
Want
Love
When
It's
Hard
to
Hold?

Do you
Want
Peace
When
It's
left
to
Unfold?

Norma Beversdorf-Rezits

Wisdom's
Unquestionably
good.
Solomon
did well
by all
his wives.

Norma Beversdorf-Rezits

I like the bite
The edgy piece
Of man, To light
The most, the
Greater part of
Him.

Norma Beversdorf-Rezits

A woman
Waits
Forever
On the brink
of life
and through
its depth;
What she
Learns
from
Waiting
Creates her
Peculiarity.

Norma Beversdorf-Rezits

I'm
so easy
to please
I ask
for nothing
but
all
you
can
give.

Norma Beversdorf-Rezits

What is
Love of life
Except
a desire
to capture
and
extend
a
moment
of
Eternity.

Norma Beversdorf-Rezits

will I presume

Beyond faith's measured grace
To think a casual name
Declares unmeasured waves?

or
am I
logical
(oh fated fault)

I'll burrow blind
A deeper path
Where you – so kindly
Blow my mind.

Norma Beversdorf-Rezits

Sentence me
into eternity
and I'll go
without a word

Norma Beversdorf-Rezits

Norma Beversdorf-Rezits

I borrowed
bringing
more than
buying
ever lends.
Refracted
light so
bends, to
give.

Norma Beversdorf-Rezits

From skillfully selected
pains spring ripples of
laughter insane – Ah
lovely sans apology
still gaining while
rolling away

Norma Beversdorf-Rezits

Norma Beversdorf-Rezits

The last breath
A spirit's bequest:
The art of penetration
Unhampered by
Limbs or eye.
A new communion
Released from
Physical limitation;
Life fresh
To merge from one
Most touched by
Love.

Norma Beversdorf-Rezits

I love
To all
the
Extremes.

Extremes
Will adjust
If they
Must
and I, in honor
Obey.

Norma Beversdorf-Rezits

There is a quiet majesty
of simply make-believe –
a living fabled view
upon reality –
To give and give
while letting live
and living too
then's real while all
is lovely fantasy.

Norma Beversdorf-Rezits

Norma Beversdorf-Rezits

I'm pregnant with knowing
Concealing expands the form.
Belief is not
relief.

Norma Beversdorf-Rezits

A thing or two
May change the
Path of life
But things are
Tools and only
That unseen
May give the
Way of life.

Norma Beversdorf-Rezits

Norma Beversdorf-Rezits

How good to die
then find
You're still
alive.

Norma Beversdorf-Rezits

We presume
children
live
in another world
When
we say
"Let's prepare them
For ours"

Is theirs
a world
with
fantasy and fact
mixed
to a
tantalizing hue?

Then
why
transformation?

Cannot we
become
Honorary members
of this other
World?

Norma Beversdorf-Rezits

Norma Beversdorf-Rezits

Because the froth of words
obscures from us the silent
Truth,
We turn
From constant talk
To walk in
Quiet.

Norma Beversdorf-Rezits

Norma Beversdorf-Rezits

I'm distilled
into words
On a page
Without face
Sans arms
the frame
or legs.

Norma Beversdorf-Rezits

Norma Beversdorf-Rezits

Let not neglect
allow the glow
from that so
human quality
go without
respect.
For imperfection
is
the soft allure
which holds
our strangled
parts aloft –
so lending
hope, to
spring
tomorrow
            on

Norma Beversdorf-Rezits

Norma Beversdorf-Rezits

A chamber held
Within a wall
containing sparks
of Hell
and seeds
from Paradise –
Oh sweetness is
because a
blunder fell.

Norma Beversdorf-Rezits

Norma Beversdorf-Rezits

She
smothers
joy
with
pain
To
invert
then
back
again.

Norma Beversdorf-Rezits

Create
the imagery
you wish
    to see
and fling
all doubts
    to
seven winds

        then
        instantly
        stake
        claim

to softly
flow
and
there
behold
a vision,
silently.

[*continued...*]

Norma Beversdorf-Rezits

Norma Beversdorf-Rezits

[...*continued*]

So breathe
and be
when
deftly
touch
Ah yield
the breeze
to make –

O birth,
new
imagery

Norma Beversdorf-Rezits

a
whisper's
near
to one
who
hears

Norma Beversdorf-Rezits

Norma Beversdorf-Rezits

Give no more
than
All you could
for giving more
than
is no good

Norma Beversdorf-Rezits

Norma Beversdorf-Rezits

You gave
Abundantly more
Than I had
Known to lend
Before.

Was I to
Know
Your ease
In giving
Surged from
Rooted laws
Decreed by
You
and
Meted
Down
To all
Who cross
Your path?

Norma Beversdorf-Rezits

He lives in a formula
so easy to perceive
and all who ever
greet him swim
equally at ease.

So simple his measure
so straight in
sterile pleasure,
Oh to be a
statue in the breeze.

Norma Beversdorf-Rezits

Norma Beversdorf-Rezits

Please
Don't explain
All away
Let someone
Grow into
Faith all the
Way.

Norma Beversdorf-Rezits

Norma Beversdorf-Rezits

Say not
those things
I should not
know, but
lend small
hints to
fuel my soul
as I
unknowing
grow.

Norma Beversdorf-Rezits

Norma Beversdorf-Rezits

I read
To forget.
I write
To know.
You look
To learn,
And win
To wait.

Norma Beversdorf-Rezits

Norma Beversdorf-Rezits

Push and force
into a mold
Unbending
Placing strength
Where faith has
Ended.
Expect full truth
And honor here
When bullets cold
Hover near
And outside
Somewhere
Freedom's flying
Holding courtship
Without trying.

Norma Beversdorf-Rezits

Norma Beversdorf-Rezits

Do tiny threads
Divide
Good and bad
To blind a sage?
Or one
Divide
A hundred ways
That long
For unity?
A moment's grace –
But
Is not
Peace
More lovely
After
War?

Norma Beversdorf-Rezits

With light of day
I see the truth
Yet still there's
Nothing I can do.

Norma Beversdorf-Rezits

Norma Beversdorf-Rezits

Where love surrounds
Even
Its lowest ebb
Flows into eternity.

Norma Beversdorf-Rezits

Norma Beversdorf-Rezits

It is another day
the sun has lent
to rain, and leaves
begin their turn –
Sink in sweet day,
to hold soft
beauty free,
and blink
tomorrow's
(autumnal)
Spring –
The now is all
So all there is –

To be as now,
soft loving
rain, to
come
and
come
again.

Norma Beversdorf-Rezits

Courtesies
So nice
Require
Hot spice
For life.

Norma Beversdorf-Rezits

Norma Beversdorf-Rezits

To behold
Rare beauty
Strong and
Deep, gives
Eternity
to all
We meet.

Norma Beversdorf-Rezits

He married a devil
But he'll never know
He married a dream
And won't let go.

Norma Beversdorf-Rezits

Norma Beversdorf-Rezits

I skin myself
Alive and
Wonder why
When all is
Neatly
Laid before
My eyes.

Norma Beversdorf-Rezits

Norma Beversdorf-Rezits

Asleep we live in our eternity
Awake we stumble haltingly
Between arousal meeting dreams
We come to being we.

Norma Beversdorf-Rezits

Norma Beversdorf-Rezits

a plunge –
body in life
leaving soul
behind,
another high
with spirit
parting frame –

together meet
together remain

soft light
shadows fall
falling making
newness aware
true, untrue

body moving
soul flexing
in sympathy

[*continued...*]

Norma Beversdorf-Rezits

Norma Beversdorf-Rezits

[*...continued*]

spirit moves
pieces too –
oh aching
parts which
ride the crests
and fall
behind where
spirit never
rests, soaring
past a human
stream so
sweet, awaiting
free.

Norma Beversdorf-Rezits

Norma Beversdorf-Rezits

What is memory
But a dream
Inverted.

Norma Beversdorf-Rezits

Norma Beversdorf-Rezits

.

It was
my pleasure
once
to decorate
and adorn –
Yet now
I wish
to hide
myself
from me
Invisibly
transform
to spirituality

yet

I am
reminded
constantly
of me
and bump
into
myself
avoiding
chance
community.

Norma Beversdorf-Rezits

Norma Beversdorf-Rezits

I respect
the right
to privacy
Yet so
much of me
is public
property.

Norma Beversdorf-Rezits

Would I enclose myself
Into a shell, withdrawing
All when someone stabs
An open wound, or
Could I still
Accept new pain
Because I know
How all began.

Norma Beversdorf-Rezits

Norma Beversdorf-Rezits

I hold
That hope
Unlocks
a mountain
of infinity.

Norma Beversdorf-Rezits

Norma Beversdorf-Rezits

Though his body
Be chained in a cave
His spirit soars higher
Than flight of eagles.
Though held as captive
A community of souls
Lifts beyond tomorrow.

Would you welcome the den
And like him dare seek
Light born of death
Which is light everlasting
Conceived by frames
Eventually consumes
To give life more room?

Norma Beversdorf-Rezits

Norma Beversdorf-Rezits

For seams
of anguish
Nobody cares
But from
its fruits
All would
Share.

Norma Beversdorf-Rezits

Norma Beversdorf-Rezits

How long are warmly
wrapped the words
dried, yet alive,

And why is life
the best when
imperfection's
never let to
rest –

Do weighted
words, pull
light, like
air, to wing
and stretch
so wide?

{*continued...*]

Norma Beversdorf-Rezits

Norma Beversdorf-Rezits

[...*continued*]

Then why
do
wordless
ways
embrace
and
linger
more
when
days
removed
they sink
to space?

Norma Beversdorf-Rezits

Norma Beversdorf-Rezits

Speak not of
But show in
Soft simplicity
the meaning of.

Norma Beversdorf-Rezits

Norma Beversdorf-Rezits

The well-turned phrase
Like the well-turned limb
Attracts
But does not win.

Norma Beversdorf-Rezits

Norma Beversdorf-Rezits

In constant awareness
Of great intervention
To cover a measure
Of quiet communication
I choose without reason
A faith, a treasure.

Norma Beversdorf-Rezits

Norma Beversdorf-Rezits

Only when
I have to
Do I do
What I
Should.

Norma Beversdorf-Rezits

Can ever
I be
All (of me)
Complete?
So
Apparent
In particles
To all
I meet.
For some
Prefer
Small parts
and leave
the whole
Unknown.
A glance
creates
a fleeting
thought
to float
a whim
to store.

Norma Beversdorf-Rezits

Norma Beversdorf-Rezits

When now
I am
only pen
in hand
without
myself,
a person
to be
what's on
a page
the pen
contrives.

Norma Beversdorf-Rezits

Norma Beversdorf-Rezits

My pride
begun
where first
it was
undone.

Norma Beversdorf-Rezits

Norma Beversdorf-Rezits

I never gave
I only got
So now
These swollen parts
Should empty
Quite a lot.

Norma Beversdorf-Rezits

Norma Beversdorf-Rezits

Dualism's the Devil
But what Light
Can Hell Create!

Norma Beversdorf-Rezits

Norma Beversdorf-Rezits

I've
scratched
a crevice
for my
life
As I
intend
to die
alive.

Norma Beversdorf-Rezits

Norma Beversdorf-Rezits

Suppose The End
as curtain's close
While I inside
Become alive
Behold
to be
as
cloistered
turned
ubiquity.

Norma Beversdorf-Rezits

Norma Beversdorf-Rezits

Obviously
    I cracked it
    I ate it
    I laid it.

Bonjour!

Norma Beversdorf-Rezits

Index of First Lines

Norma Beversdorf-Rezits

Acknowledgments

Profound thanks to my sister, Paula Beversdorf Gabbard for cataloging and indexing Mom's poetry diary, seven folders and three chapbooks. Thanks also to my brother-in-law Krin Gabbard for his thoughtful and detailed editing, and for his enthusiasm and selection advice. Warm thanks to my friend Daniel Burton for his gentle and erudite editorial wisdom. Thanks to English Professor Tom Dillingham for his advice on textual aesthetics, and to my friends, Martha Ward and Karen Robison for their unflagging support and knowledge. Special gratitude to George Hunter Hutton, the artist who kindly allowed the use of his work on the book's cover. Knowing I have such skilled, thoughtful, and supportive friends contributed to the joy of this project.

The greatest acknowledgment of all goes to our mother, Norma Beversdorf-Rezits, who was a model for love, independence, wisdom, intelligence and wit. We were lucky to have her.

Anne Beversdorf

Made in the USA
Coppell, TX
04 January 2022

70798890R00090